M000014354

Guided Journal

A LITTLE BIT OF

MINDFULNESS

Guided Journal

A LITTLE BIT OF
MINDFULNESS

YOUR PERSONAL PATH
TO AWARENESS

AMY LEIGH MERCREE

STERLING ETHOS
New York

THIS BOOK BELONGS TO

_____

_____

_____

STERLING ETHOS
New York

An Imprint of Sterling Publishing Co., Inc.
1166 Avenue of the Americas
New York, NY 10036

ISBN 978-1-4549-4033-3

Portions of this publication previously published as *A Little Bit of Mindfulness.*

Distributed in Canada by Sterling Publishing Co., Inc.
c/o Canadian Manda Group, 664 Annette Street
Toronto, Ontario M6S 2C8, Canada
Distributed in the United Kingdom by GMC Distribution Services
Castle Place, 166 High Street, Lewes, East Sussex BN7 1XU, England
Distributed in Australia by NewSouth Books
University of New South Wales, Sydney, NSW 2052, Australia

For information about custom editions, special sales, and premium and corporate purchases,
please contact Sterling Special Sales at 800-805-5489 or specialsales@sterlingpublishing.com.

Manufactured in Singapore

2 4 6 8 10 9 7 5 3 1

sterlingpublishing.com

Cover design by Elizabeth Mihaltse Lindy
Interior design by Sharon Jacobs

❈ CONTENTS ❧

INTRODUCTION

Mindfulness has become a popular buzzword in the last several years. But it's so much more than a trendy hashtag. It's an opportunity to deepen your experience of reality and live a life of meaning and fulfillment.

The concept of mindfulness is all about being present, fully in the moment, and becoming aware of yourself and your surroundings. It also means practicing nonreactivity; that is, not becoming overwhelmed by your environment. Celebrities, scientists, athletes, and people from all walks of life tout the amazing physical and mental benefits of mindfulness, and scientific research backs up many of their experiences. Incredibly, studies have shown that daily mindfulness practices can reduce cortisol, the stress hormone in our bodies, by more than 50 percent.

The practice of mindfulness exists in many cultures, but the North American practice of mindfulness was popularized by Jon Kabat-Zinn in the 1960s. While traveling in Asia, he became a master practitioner of mindfulness and meditation. He brought his experiences back to the United States and created Mindfulness-Based Stress Reduction (MBSR), which remains popular to this day.

Mindfulness isn't just for the rich and famous—people all over the world have taken it up in an effort to understand themselves and function better in modern life. Each and every one of us can learn something from the meditative practice, which has been around for thousands of years. If you are among the many who are searching for a way to increase your quality of life, look no further.

THIS JOURNAL

You will learn about your own mindfulness and being present with the others around you with the information in this book. It can be used on its own, or in conjunction with *A Little Bit of Mindfulness*, which includes more in-depth information on some of the material in this book.

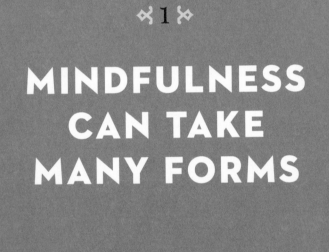

❖ 1 ❖

MINDFULNESS CAN TAKE MANY FORMS

WHETHER YOU ARE A BEGINNER OR AN EXPERT, you will find many types of mindfulness that can expand your awareness. Mindful practices such as meditation and yoga have been scientifically proven to improve physical health, reduce anxiety, and enhance happiness. So, wherever you are on your journey, even if you've never practiced mindfulness before, try one of these relaxing exercises today.

Mini-moments of mindfulness practice can be done any time throughout the day and require no special training or ability. They are a great place to start for beginners who want to incorporate mindfulness in small pieces.

MINDFUL SEEING

Not all mindful activities require closing your eyes—in fact, some people may feel more comfortable being able to take in visual stimuli while they meditate. The only requirement for mindful seeing is a window with a view. Do this meditation for ten to twenty minutes.

These are the five steps to mindful seeing:

1. Find a comfortable place in front of a window with a view.

2. Carefully observe everything while looking out the window. Try not to label what you see. Instead, simply notice colors, patterns, and textures.

3. Pay attention to anything that moves—wind blowing leaves, people walking, birds flying. Pay attention to the many different shapes you can see through the window. Let yourself view everything from the perspective of someone unfamiliar with what you are seeing.

4. Be closely observant but do not judge what you see. Don't fixate on or critique the sights you see. Simply be aware of them.

5. Any time your attention strays, redirect it nonjudgmentally by noticing another color or movement. Don't let distractions pull you away from observing; just gently pull your mind back.

THE BLUEBERRY EXERCISE

The blueberry exercise is a great beginner's mindfulness practice. Usually, a facilitator provides practitioners with a blueberry and requests that they pretend they have never seen one before. The facilitator tells the practitioners to pay close attention to how the blueberry looks, how it feels in their hands, how its skin changes after being touched and held, how it smells, and how it tastes. By focusing on a single small object, practitioners use this mindfulness practice to help focus on what's in front of them and give all their attention to the present moment. The blueberry exercise forces practitioners to stay in the moment completely.

LOVING-KINDNESS MEDITATION

Loving-kindness is a mindfulness practice that connects practitioners to the outside world by sending and receiving love. The steps of a short loving-kindness meditation follow.

1. Close your eyes, sit in a comfortable position with your back upright, and relax your body. Focus inward. Take a deep breath in and then back.

2. To receive loving-kindness, think of someone who loves you and cares about you. It could be anyone in your life, past or present. Imagine that person on your right, sending you love, and then feel the warmth and goodwill coming from a different person who loves you on your left. Then move your focus outward, imagining you are surrounded by people who care for you on all sides. Bask in the warmth of this feeling.

3. To send loving-kindness, bring your attention back to the first person you visualized on your right side. Start to send the positivity you feel back to that person. You can repeat the following mantra to send loving-kindness:

MAY ALL PEOPLE BE HAPPY.

MAY ALL PEOPLE BE FREE.

MAY ALL PEOPLE BE HEALTHY.

MAY ALL PEOPLE BE AT PEACE.

A good order for your mindfulness practice is to send loving-kindness to those you love, then to send it to a neutral person you may visualize. And, to finish your exercise, send it to all beings in the world.

BODY-SCAN MEDITATION

Popularized by Jon Kabat-Zinn, founder of the MBSR movement who we mentioned earlier, a body scan is a simple but effective way to practice mindfulness. It is accessible to beginners and does not require much time. The body scan moves through each region of the body and asks participants to pay special attention to how the parts of their body are feeling. The scan traditionally moves from the toes up to the legs, pelvic region, abdomen, chest, back, shoulders, hands, arms, neck, and face/head. These are the five main steps of the body-scan meditation:

1. Lie on your back, with your palms facing the ceiling and your feet placed slightly apart. If you are unable to lie down, sit in a comfortable chair with your feet solidly on the floor.

2. Remain very still for the duration of the exercise and move only if necessary and with awareness of your movements.

3. Begin with a guided portion of the body scan. First, bring your awareness to your breathing and observe the way your breath flows in and out. By noticing the rhythm of breath, you can relax into your breathing

more fully. The goal in breath awareness is not to change the way you are breathing but to hold gentle awareness of it. As you relax, your breath will likely change and become deeper and steadier naturally.

4. Next, begin to pay attention to your body: how your clothes feel against your skin, how the surface you are sitting or lying on feels, how the temperature of the room affects you, and what is going on in the environment around you.

5. Last, guide your awareness to any particular parts of your body that call attention to themselves—these could be places that are sore or feel very heavy or that feel light or perhaps are tingling. Bring your awareness upward from the toes to the legs, pelvic region, abdomen, chest, back, and shoulders, and then to the hands, arms, neck, and face/head. Note places where you may not feel anything at all or, on the other end of the spectrum, that are greatly sensitive.

Once participants have completed the scan, they can come back to the room by slowly opening their eyes and moving to a comfortable sitting position.

TONGLEN

Tonglen is a Tibetan Buddhist meditation practice that literally translates to "giving and taking." The practice was originally described in seven steps and is attributed to an Indian Buddhist teacher, Atisha Dipankara Shrijnana. Langri Tangpa wrote them down for the first time in the eleventh century. The practice involves breathing exercises you can perform while sitting and that are used to purify your karma by training you in altruism, and reducing selfish attachment.

During your practice, breathe in and visualize taking in others' suffering as well as your own. This suffering can be about a particular group of people, a specific country, or even just one person. When you breathe out, give recognition and compassion to all living beings. Pema Chödrön, well-known American Buddhist nun and author, instructs practitioners to breathe out and hold space for others' hearts and minds to feel great enough to live with their discomfort and suffering. She suggests that if your practice is for those without food, breathe out food. If your practice is on behlaf those without homes, breathe out shelter. The in breath is your wish to take away suffering, and the out breath is your wish to send comfort and happiness to the suffering people (or countries, animals, etc.). The idea behind tonglen is that practitioners can develop and expand their loving-kindness.

The following mindfulnesss practice can help to soothe your mind but do so through thoughtful physical activity. Don't be taken aback by the fact that they are exercises—both can be scaled back for beginners and offer various levels of intensity.

QIGONG

Qigong is an ancient Chinese exercise and health system that involves body posture, movement, breathing, and meditation. It began as a traditional philosophy for spiritual well-being but has transitioned into a health and mindfulness exercise as well. The first step of qigong is to train your breathing so you can focus on a relaxed, rhythmic breathing pattern. Qigong also encourages the stretching of your breath, which means holding your inhales and your exhales to expand them. Qigong has mental elements and instills the importance of settling the mind and relaxing physically and mentally. There are specific sets of movements that can be completed in qigong, as well as various postures (standing, sitting, lying down) for those who wish to delve deeper into the practice.

TAI CHI

Tai chi is another ancient Chinese exercise, actually a martial art form that is sometimes called meditation in motion. It promotes relaxation, stress relief, lowered anxiety, and heightened awareness. Tai chi practices are a series of slow, methodical movements that are low impact and can be incorporated into any mindfulness routine.

The most important step in tai chi is warming up the body, which promotes mental relaxation. A good place to begin is with a loosening-up exercise. While standing with your feet parallel, relax your arms at your sides and begin rotating to the left and then to right, allowing your arms to hang loosely. This can be expanded to your neck, shoulders, and spine so that your whole body begins to warm up before you move into your exercise regimen.

One of the most basic tai chi movements that encourages flexibility is the windmill. With your feet placed apart and parallel, relax your shoulders and point your fingers toward the floor. On the inhale, lift your arms over your head straight above your shoulders, and stretch toward the ceiling while arching your back. On the exhale, bend forward slowly and move your hands down the midline of your body. Then bend forward from the hips and allow your arms to hang loosely in front of you. When you inhale again, return to your starting position.

After reading about all these different techniques, which one(s) appeal to you the most? What parts of each practice do you find enticing?

When you try any of the practices, write about your experiences below.

When you did the loving-kindness meditation, what sensations did you
notice in your body? Where?

_____

_____

_____

_____

_____

_____

_____

_____

_____

_____

_____

_____

_____

_____

_____

_____

_____

When you tried the body-scan meditation, how did you feel afterward? What is the difference between how you felt before the meditation and after?

Did you enjoy the blueberry exercise? Did you find it challenging to bring your focus to such a singular experience and keep it there?

Think of some practical ways to increase your ability to be mindful on a daily basis. (Some examples may be turning off your phone at night or spending more time in nature.)

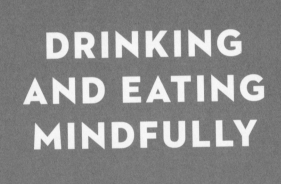

❖ 2 ❖

DRINKING AND EATING MINDFULLY

EATING MINDFULLY IS INCREDIBLY POWERFUL. Many people have complicated relationships with food. We are often eating while stressed, and rushing from one activity to the next. Physically, this kind of eating is challenging for our bodies. When we are rushed or stressed, our bodies are using energy to hold tension and this activates our stress responses. The energy used to hold tension in the body can cause us to digest our food improperly. That in turn can contribute to digestive issues and immune diseases.

As you eat, you should chew your food thoroughly. Chewing assiduously is the first step in the process of digestion and the most commonly neglected. We need to produce copious amounts of saliva during this stage for proper digestion to take place.

Also, many people do not realize that drinking too quickly—even healthy smoothies—may not allow you to absorb all of the nutrients. That is why some dieticians recommend you "chew" your smoothie. When you drink a smoothie, take the time to chew it. Taste the flavors of the smoothie and allow your senses to come alive. During this process, your mouth will salivate and assist in proper digestion.

We often do not take time to appreciate and love our food. By intentionally loving our food and putting a positive intention into enjoying what we are eating, we ultimately give ourselves more energy from our food. Mindless eating means that we are detached from our food and our hunger indicators, and that we are not present with our bodies or our food. Mindless eating is much more common than mindful eating. In fact, our culture encourages mindless eating. We go out for dinner and chat with our friends without taking the time to tune in with our bodies. This can lead to overeating and ignoring the indicators that the body gives us when we are full. Aim for eating to live, rather than living to eat.

We often choose to eat in an attempt to fill an emotional void. But sometimes we are not consciously choosing to eat. We simply find ourselves eating without intentionally choosing to. Instead of noticing hunger, we notice sadness or boredom. Because we naturally get a surge of dopamine (a natural substance in our bodies that improves the pumping strength of the heart and improves blood flow to the kidneys) when we eat, we are drawn to food. Eating makes us feel good. But there are healthier ways to achieve this same feeling than mindless eating.

When we eat as we do other things, we are eating mindlessly. Many of us eat our lunch at our desk or while browsing social media. This is not eating mindfully. We become disconnected from the sensations of tasting and digesting.

Mindful eating is partially about consciously choosing what you will eat. It is about stopping when cravings hit, to consider the choice to eat or not. It is about listening to what the body needs and honoring that. If you are hungry, eat. If you are not, then don't. Slow down and let your body have time to communicate what you need as you eat.

Think about choosing to eat a blueberry muffin. First, you notice you are hungry and craving something sweet. You pass ice cream stores and fast-food restaurants. You notice an organic bakery. You choose to give your body something sweet that also has nutrients, so you enter the organic bakery. You notice a blueberry muffin made from locally sourced blueberries and sweetened with maple syrup. You choose to buy the muffin because you believe it is the healthiest choice for your body. You look at the muffin. You notice the swirls of blue and how different areas of the muffin are baked. You silently thank the people who have prepared the muffin, including those who grew the ingredients that are in it. You break open the muffin. You notice its texture. You smell the aroma of maple syrup, blueberries, and fresh bread. You take one bite and feel your mouth respond with excitement. With gratitude, you slowly chew and experience each bite. You intentionally choose when to swallow. You feel the muffin travel into your esophagus and downward to your stomach. You take your time to eat the muffin in this intentional manner until you notice your stomach beginning to feel full. If you feel full before you finish the muffin, give yourself the opportunity to save the rest for later, when your body cues you that you are hungry once again.

Eating mindfully is something you can do at every meal. Eating can become a meditation when you sit down to refuel your body with food or drink.

MINDFUL EATING MEDITATION

1. First, notice when your body is signaling that you are hungry. Take a few deep breaths. Pay attention to these sensations and understand that they are hunger cues. Breathe and accept this feeling. Do not react by eating immediately when you notice hunger. Then, choose to nourish yourself with healthy food.

2. Become aware of the food choices you have. Notice the thoughts and feelings that come up as you consider these choices. Stop yourself and breathe. Make a choice that is aligned with what your body needs based on your energy level, the intensity of your hunger, and the activities planned for the day. Notice which choices appeal only as emotional comfort.

3. Prepare your food mindfully, or if the food is being prepared for you, consider the preparation of the food and visualize this process. In either case, consider how the food gets to your plate. Consider where it comes from and how it was prepared.

4. Notice the textures in the food. As you prepare your food, mindfully cut each vegetable or remove each wrapper with care and with purpose. Notice each sense as you smell, observe, and feel the food during preparation. Observe your mouth as it begins to salivate as you prepare to eat.

5. Sit down at a designated place to eat. Set your food in front of you and take a moment to connect with your meal. See the colors and shapes of your food. Set aside any distractions. Turn off the TV. Put away your phone. Sit comfortably but with good posture. Connect with your breath. Enjoy the silence.

6. Place the first bite into your mouth. Focus your awareness on the senses of smell, taste, and touch as the food brushes your tongue. Begin to chew and continue to breathe.

7. Chew all the food in your mouth thoroughly before choosing to swallow. Create space between chewing and the intention to swallow. Try to transform swallowing from an unconscious reflex to an intentional process.

8. Stay present. Use your breath. If you are creating mental lists or are absent from the moment, unconscious patterns of eating will reemerge. Do not judge yourself if this happens. Bring yourself back using your breath and the awareness of your senses.

9. Check in with your body to notice cues for fullness. If your stomach feels three-quarters full, this is a good time to stop eating. Do not let the amount of food in front of you determine how much you eat. Let your body indicate what it needs and when it needs it.

10. As you finish eating, notice the tastes that linger in your mouth. Feel the fullness in your stomach. Notice any changes from previous meals and make a mental note of hunger and fullness cues that may be new to you.

Continue these practices. If possible, practice daily for twenty-one days. Many yogis and mindfulness practitioners believe it takes this long to form new habits. The more you practice mindfulness in your daily activities, such as walking and eating, the more naturally it will occur. Mindfulness will be present. You will find yourself slowing down your mind to truly experience your life. When you experience this shift, you will not want to go back to multitasking while eating or walking. You may find that you accomplish more by focusing on each task wholly and mindfully.

Through mindful eating, you may find yourself becoming healthier, losing weight, and developing better digestion. If you already have a meditation practice, you may find these specific practices enhance your overall ability to meditate. Use this meditation to connect with your body and realize the subtle messages your body is giving that you often miss in your daily life.

Did you enjoy your food more than usual by eating it mindfully?

Are you conditioned to multitask or seek a distraction?

When you practiced the mindful eating meditation, did you find yourself wishing that you could look at your phone or watch a show?

What do you think some of the benefits of practicing mindful eating on a regular basis might be?

Do you want to try to set a goal to eat a certain number of meals per day or per week mindfully? Do you think that might be something that would increase your health and quality of life? Explain. Use the following pages to create a food journal to reflect on your goals. For more food journaling pages, refer to pages 114–133 at the end of this book.

DATE		B=BREAKFAST L=LUNCH D=DINNER S=SNACK
5/21	B	2 fried eggs, toast, and coffee
	L	Caesar Salad and Iced Tea

DATE   **B**=BREAKFAST **L**=LUNCH **D**=DINNER **S**=SNACK

DATE   **B**=BREAKFAST **L**=LUNCH **D**=DINNER **S**=SNACK

DATE   B=BREAKFAST L=LUNCH D=DINNER S=SNACK

DATE   **B**=BREAKFAST **L**=LUNCH **D**=DINNER **S**=SNACK

3

MINDFUL EMOTIONS

I N THIS CHAPTER, WE JOURNEY DEEPLY WITHIN THE
emotional body. That's the part of our being that's woven
through the physical body, and encompasses our emotions
and their energy. Our physical bodies are knit with electromagnetic
energy, and we have an electromagnetic field around us. This is often
referred to as the body's aura. The field is easily measurable.

Part of the neutral energy contained in this field is what holds
together the energy of our emotions. Our emotions are generated
within our mind and through the complex symphony of brain and
body chemicals. The emotions we experience also have electromagnetic energy and the universal life force that permeates our physical
bodies and our being.

In fact, we are all multidimensional beings. We exist in the
physical dimension, and we also exist in our own internal emotional
worlds. These parts of us interact with the invisible energy world

that is interwoven with all existence. That invisible energy world is comprised of a universal life force. This is a clear, clean, neutral energy that enlivens all existence. Some people like to characterize this energy as love or light. It's both these things and more. It's the universality that weaves us together.

Endeavoring to be mindful in our emotional life is probably the biggest challenge for human beings. As humans, we are an emotional bunch! No matter whether we repress emotions or are exquisitely in tune with them, we are governed by them in large portions of our lives. So, to bring the skill of being mindful into our emotional experience is a useful way to become more self-actualized. It also brings us a sense of calm and tranquility that we often crave, especially when our emotions are agitated.

For this meditation, we invoke an ancient Taoist goddess named Change'E. In Chinese mythology, she is thought to live within the moon and to be a nurturing and caring presence. She is uniquely attuned to our emotions and also incredibly adept at helping us navigate their symbolism while easily surfing their ebbs and flows.

EMOTIONAL CALM MEDITATION

Take a few minutes to relax. Close your eyes and spend some time being mindful of your breath. Allow yourself to enter a meditative state. When you have quieted your mind enough that you are beginning to feel space between your thoughts, begin the following process:

1. Bring your attention to the center of your chest. This is the place where many cultures and philosophies maintain that the energy of the heart resides. This energy center is an origin point for universal love.

2. Center your attention in your chest, allowing yourself to feel a pulsing sensation there. Allow yourself to imagine that universal love energy is pulsing.

3. Use this as the access point from which you will process and integrate your emotions today. As you keep your attention centered in your chest, say aloud or in your mind, "*For my highest good and the highest good of all life, I call upon Chang'E to help me balance and integrate my emotions so I may live in ever-growing harmony and joy.*"

4. Rest now, with your eyes closed, and place your hands in the following mudra: connect the tips of your thumbs with the outermost knuckle of your ring fingers on the side closest to your middle fingers. (*Note:* A mudra is a hand movement, position, or gesture used in ceremonies and in yoga to enhance meditation; each mudra has a specific meaning and can be healing or bring a particular energetic vibration.)

5. Inhale deeply through your nose and feel the motion all the way down into your abdomen, filling it completely with air. Place your tongue on the roof of your mouth. Exhale the air through your mouth in a steady slow stream, as if you are blowing the breath through a straw. Do this two more times.

6. Gently the point three times where your thumbs are resting. Now, with your tongue on the roof of your mouth, sit for several minutes and allow the stored emotions within you to process through you. You don't need to know what they are about. Simply sit with your hands in the position described and allow your body to process. Your body stores many emotions, and you may never have access to what they are. But if you simply allow them to process through you, they can be released as is for your highest good. Stuck emotions equal poor mental and spiritual health or disease. Allowing the emotions to move equals health and vibrancy. Simply allow yourself to detox emotions at this time. You can set a timer or look at a clock and do this meditation for three to seven minutes. Just sit quietly, allowing your being to integrate and reshuffle the emotional decks within you.

7. Release your hands from the mudra after the time is up, and place them in your lap or at your sides, face up and palms open. Now, allow yourself to simply observe what you're feeling emotionally. You might feel sleepy or bored. You might feel sad or melancholic. You might feel happy or agitated. You might feel any number of other emotions. You might even be aware of fear underlying your other emotions. Just observe all of these feelings. None are good or bad. They just exist. They're just energy. They are impermanent, ever-moving, fluid energies. You can watch them and even direct them, but they're not you. You are the witness who sits and simply watches the inner show. Allow yourself to mindfully observe your emotions. Sometimes, you can let the part of yourself that is like a wise parent participate. That's the part that might tell you ways to calm and quiet your emotions and care for yourself in a more loving manner. Even that is simply an aspect of you to be witnessed by the one who is behind it all, who is ever neutral, and ever at peace. This is your true self.

How did it feel to tap into your emotional presence during this meditation?

Were you able to observe your emotions without judgment?

When you brought your attention to the center of your chest, did you notice a feeling or sensation there? A pulsing or tingling? A warmth or coolness?

When you brought your attention to that heart center in your chest, did you feel any emotion? What thoughts popped into your mind as you brought your conscious awareness there?

Did tapping into your emotions and becoming more consciously aware of them make you feel any greater degree of comfort or emotional safety?

Did this meditation bring up anything that you feel you needed to clear from your physical body and from your emotional body? If so, is there anything else you could do that might help that process along? (For example, vigorous physical exercise, talking to a close friend about your feelings, neural feedback, or even therapy.)

❖ 4 ❖

MINDFUL
RELATIONSHIPS

THE PURPOSE OF PRACTICING MINDFULNESS IS not just to achieve a feeling of calmness. It is to improve your quality of life. When you're able to cultivate a more mindful approach to your day, you are able to be fully present in whatever you're doing. When you're able to be completely present, you're often drastically more effective, whether at accomplishing a task, interacting with somebody, or generating a new idea. Complete and utter presence and mindfulness may be the keys to peak performance.

In the dance of intimacy, the concept of bringing mindfulness into relationships is a valuable one to consider. If you're able to bring mindfulness, for example, to your romantic relationships, imagine how they might be different. What if you were able to be 100 percent present with your partner and yourself during any given exchange of love, caring, passion, or even conflict?

How many times during a disagreement with a significant other are you thinking ahead to what you're going to say next instead of being mindful and listening to what your partner is trying to express? It is part of human nature to try to defend ourselves when we're feeling attacked. It's also human nature to lash out or exhibit certain behaviors when we feel threatened, either physically or emotionally. When we have a disagreement with somebody we care about, we often feel less safe. We feel like a piece of our emotional health might be impacted because of the dissension.

Throw our neurotic inner voice into the mix during any given exchange, and we have a whole chaotic narrative in our own minds. Then we miss the opportunity to be present and listen to our partner. You can see how being mindful during times of strife in a relationship could be valuable; we would be more available to validate our partner's feelings and come to mutual agreement about troublesome issues.

What about during the good times or just the neutral times? How often have we missed the full depth and scope of peak experiences because we were distracted by our mind's urge to multitask? Imagine you're parasailing with your partner. You're attached to parachutes floating high above the water. Below you, sunlight glints off the surface of a sparkling sea, green turtles swimming in the waves. It's easy to be more present in that moment because it's novel. But if it's not a peak experience, are you ever 100 percent present and mindful in the moment? How frequently? Take an inventory of how present you're able to stay in your relationships—and not just in romantic relationships. Think about the last conversation you had with a friend. How frequently did your mind wander?

The ultimate enemy of mindfulness today is the smartphone. How many times do you see people having dinner together and at least one person is on the phone, looking utterly engaged in whatever they're texting or doing. This is at the expense of presence with the other people. And there's no judgment here, because most of us have done it. And we will probably do it again. But when we bring awareness to our level of mindfulness, we have an opportunity to make a conscious choice to change it. Practicing mindfulness and meditation on a regular basis gives us access to more ability to be present. And then it is our choice if we want to tap into that ability.

MINDFUL RELATIONSHIPS MEDITATION

You can use this meditation to increase your ability to stay present and be mindful during relationship-based interactions. It is like weight lifting for the mind and heart.

In a relationship, any interaction is really one of the heart. Whether you define the heart as the organ that pumps your blood, the emotional energy center in your chest, or the complicated chemical symphony coursing through your body, love is truly the core of the matter.

In this meditation, we embrace the heart and invite it to feel emotionally safe and nurtured. When the heart feels safe, it lessens the likelihood of emotional distractions that may take us outside of our focused presence. In Greek mythology, the goddess Aphrodite was known to govern love, pleasure, relationships, matters of the heart, and romantic unions. We invite her archetype to school us in how to have mindful, harmonious, joyous relationships of all kinds.

Find a comfortable place for this meditation. Make sure you will be undisturbed for fifteen to thirty minutes. This is a wonderful meditation to do lying down, if you are able. You want to allow yourself to relax deeply during this process.

1. Spend a few minutes focusing on your breath as it comes in and goes out of your mouth or nose. Feel the sensation of air moving and passing through. Notice how it feels as it goes deeper into your lungs and how it feels as you blow it out as slowly as you can. Bring your focus to that air and try to fill your lungs like two balloons. What if you could fully inflate them? What might that feel like? Bring the breath deeply into the base of your lungs, all the way down. When you exhale, feel your lung tissue being revitalized. Feel the fresh air you're bringing in oxygenate your body, and feel the carbon dioxide and other components of the air as you blow out. Feel yourself letting go of that which you no longer need.

2. In Chinese medicine, the lungs are considered the storehouse for grief energy. Deep breathing is one of the most effective ways to gently and easily let go of deep-seated grief. We all have grief in our hearts and in our lungs. Whether for specific life events or, more frequently, for things in our world or the world around us, it's a natural part of being human. But if we can mitigate that grief energy, help it to flow, and let it go just as easily as it was acquired, we give ourselves the opportunity to have a more open heart and to feel greater levels of emotional freedom.

3. Use the power of deep breathing even as you're walking to work or grabbing groceries at the supermarket. Do some deep breathing to oxygenate and cleanse your lungs physically as well as to release emotional energy from them. Let go of the emotional energy that is stored there, easily and gently through breathing.

4. Relationships are a dance of energy and light steeped down to physical, nonphysical, verbal, emotional, and mental interactions of every kind. But in the most basic sense, any interaction with another person, animal, or plant is an exchange of energy.

5. So, as you feel yourself in this restful meditative place, contemplate, without judgment, the interactions that you have with people. Specifically, focus on the romantic relationships. Allow yourself to see, feel, and know which interactions and energy exchanges enhance you, which are neutral, and which deplete you. Simply notice this information. There is no pressure to take action on it now. It simply exists.

6. Now invite the benevolent, life-affirming presence of the archetypal goddess Aphrodite into your meditation by stating the following internally or aloud: *"I ask that all that transpires in this meditation be for the very highest good of all life and in accordance with universal natural law, helping all and harming none. I ask that the goddess Aphrodite infuse the room and space in which I am meditating right now with her loving, ecstatic light. I now decree that my relationships will be harmonious, fulfilling, joyful, and full of infinite, unconditional love. I commit to being present in my relationships. I invite my relationship partners to do the same with great love and care. It is done."*

7. Remember that love is free. It transcends space and time. It does not require physical proximity. Love is an ever-flowing energy and yet it is also tangible and intangible, imaginative and real, particles and waves. Love is an infinite paradox because it is all things. We live in a paradoxical universe, and love is the energy that powers it.

8. Contemplate the infinite nature of love as you use the word *love* like a mantra. Simply repeat it internally as you meditate. Whenever your mind wanders, simply say the word *love*. Allow yourself to notice each time you say the word *love*; what it evokes. What do you feel? Do you envision a certain color? A picture? Do you think of a certain person? Do you hear a song or sound in your mind when you say the word *love* within yourself? Do you smell fragrant roses or blooming jasmine? What is love for you on a sensory level? Let this awareness bubble up with no effort on your part. Allow yourself to rest in an infinite ocean of love. Float on its surface in complete relaxation and surrender to the infinite reality that is the truth of existence. You are love.

9. When you are ready, bring your attention back into your body and into the room. Feel yourself present in this reality. Use your hands to rub your feet, legs, arms, and shoulders and say aloud, "I am here now. I am present." Make sure you drink plenty of water. It is important to be well hydrated after you meditate because your body may be engaging in self-healing as a result, and proper hydration can aid in the process.

The essence of infinite love with which you connected will help you feel a greater level of internal safety. And the intention to be present and mindful in your relationships will gently permeate your life.

Have you ever been more attentive to your smartphone than to someone with whom you are having dinner?

_____

_____

_____

_____

_____

_____

_____

Have you been on the other end of that equation? And been with somebody sharing a meal or sharing space and wishing they would put down their phone and engage with you?

_____

_____

_____

_____

_____

_____

More thoughts on consciously engaging . . .

During the meditation, when you tapped into your heart and reviewed your romantic relationships, which ones enhanced you, were neutral, or eventually depleted you? List them here.

_____

_____

_____

_____

_____

_____

_____

_____

_____

_____

_____

_____

_____

_____

_____

_____

Using this list, write down one to three words that describe that particular relationship.

What conclusions can you draw about creating a life of emotional

well-being, safety, and pleasure for yourself using this insight?

When you focused on the word *love* and let it permeate your being,

what did that feel like?

※ 5 ※

OBSERVING YOUR THOUGHTS

USING YOUR AWARENESS TO WATCH YOUR MIND is another tool for reaching a deeper meditative state. Sometimes this type of meditation is referred to as insight meditation. It can often be the next step in watching the breath. After you have calmed the mind to focus on the breath, you can continue to notice the thoughts that come. It is believed, particularly by Buddhists, that this deep type of insight meditation is the path to enlightenment. The trick to this process is a nonjudgmental attitude. We do not judge ourselves for having thoughts. We do not attach ourselves or our identity to our thoughts. We create a separation between the mind and the observer. The true self is not the mind, neither is it the body. The true self is the observer. The true self is the silent witness of the mind. The true self is stillness. Its form is omnipresent light.

It is believed that through this meditation, the Buddha achieved enlightenment. Without aiming for this outcome, we can still receive many benefits from this practice. We can experience improved health by reducing levels of stress and anxiety and, ultimately, have more restful sleep. We can begin to observe the inner processes of the mind, allowing us to follow our thoughts and to notice how thoughts can become a chain reaction when we do not have intentional mindfulness. We can slow those thoughts down, reducing the mental chatter and creating a quiet mind. Many people notice that they become more connected to others through compassion, more connected to the living world around them, and more connected to their true selves. Many experience reduction of symptoms of mood disorders such as anxiety and depression when they are able to watch their mind nonjudgmentally. You can use this meditation to practice nonattachment, which can extend to your daily life in so many ways. It can reduce your emotional reactivity and enhance your ability to carefully think before you act or speak.

WATCHING THE MIND MEDITATION

Prepare your environment by finding a quiet and comfortable place. Include anything that may help to set a relaxed atmosphere. Choose a time you would like to practice meditation and set a timer so you can let go of mentally tracking time. Start with five to ten minutes. Find a comfortable position.

1. Bring your awareness first to your breath. Breathing through your nose, exhale all the breath from your lungs, and then naturally allow the breath to flow back into your lungs through your nose. As the breath flows in, follow it with your awareness.

2. As you inhale, begin to exaggerate the belly, allowing it to expand and fill up like a big balloon. As you exhale, let the navel fall toward the spine and allow the belly to empty while exhaling completely. Begin the three-part full yogic breath. Do this by first filling your belly, then moving your breath upward to fill your rib cage, and finally allowing your chest to expand as it fills with air. Inhale deeply.

3. Now allow yourself to just be with what is. This is a time to just sit in the moment as it comes. Your only task is to breathe and be. Begin to notice your mind. If your mind is very busy, use thoughts to anchor yourself to the breath. As you inhale, tell yourself silently, "*I am not this body,*" and as you exhale, "*I am not this mind.*" This reminds you that you are not the body or the mind, you are the silent witness. You are the observer of the mind and of the breath.

4. Notice when thoughts come into your mind. Thoughts will come, and that is okay. As thoughts come, try not to fight or resist them. Try to practice nonjudgment of the thoughts. Each time you notice a thought, do just that—notice it.

5. Observe your thoughts as a continuous flow, as if you are watching waves crashing in from the ocean or clouds floating through the sky. Note each thought, and watch it go as you allow the thoughts to pass by. Notice the next thought, and watch it pass. Observe yourself noticing the thoughts as they pass. Keep paying attention to your breath as each breath comes.

6. Remember that thoughts are okay. They will come, so try not to judge them or your feelings, especially the ones you have about the fact that you are having thoughts. Notice yourself judging yourself. Notice yourself noticing yourself. Stay with the three-part full yogic breaths. Use each breath as an opportunity to fasten your mind back into the present. Use the words in step 3 that focus on inhaling and exhaling if you find your mind is wandering. Notice the wandering mind and come back to the breath.

7. Note that you are not resisting thoughts. You are observing them. You are allowing them to float by. You are curious about them but not attached to them. They do not control you. You are not your mind. Notice the stillness that may arrive. Observe the space between the thoughts. Continue noticing as long as possible or until the timer goes off. Then, allow yourself to come back very slowly and gently. Practice this meditation daily, and use this practice as a part of your daily life.

Remember: You are not your body or your mind. You are a silent witness. We can begin to deepen this understanding by using the power of the breath. We can watch ourselves breathe and observe our bodies. This helps us understand that we are separate from the body. We are watching the body. Watching the mind allows us to gain insight and go even deeper, understanding that we are not only our thoughts but we are also infinite, and we are witnessing our own existence while simultaneously living it. We are watching the mind. These two processes can help us achieve meditation.

You may find you are meditating and suddenly you have the thought, *Hey, I am meditating!* which effectively ends your blissful state of meditation. This is okay. Come back and keep observing. The space that you feel between the thoughts and the breaths is meditation. The serenity and bliss you feel between the thoughts show that you have achieved that state of meditation that allows you to feel your true essence.

Did you find yourself judging the types of thoughts that popped into your mind? Or were you able to be neutral about them? Or maybe a combination of both?

How did it feel to connect with that silent witness within you?

Was there even a single moment when you were able to rest between the thoughts moving through your mind? Did you experience a sensation or emotion when that happened?

After doing this meditation, what insight do you feel you gained about the nature of consciousness?

CONCLUSION

I hope you have enjoyed your journey into mindfulness! Human beings have endeavored to be mindful for many thousands of years. We've tried lots of different methods and now it's your turn to find what works for you. As you live each day, present to the moments and mindfully experiencing your life, I wish you joy, harmony, and happiness. May your life be filled with love!

Use the rest of this journal as a space for reflection. Detail your mindfulness practices and observe the changes that you've made over time.

XO,

Amy

DATE	TIME	EXPERIENCE

DATE	TIME	EXPERIENCE

DATE | TIME | EXPERIENCE

DATE	TIME	EXPERIENCE

DATE   TIME   EXPERIENCE

DATE	TIME	EXPERIENCE

DATE	TIME	EXPERIENCE

DATE	TIME	EXPERIENCE

DATE	TIME	EXPERIENCE

DATE   TIME   EXPERIENCE

DATE	TIME	EXPERIENCE

DATE	TIME	EXPERIENCE

DATE	TIME	EXPERIENCE

DATE	TIME	EXPERIENCE

DATE	TIME	EXPERIENCE

DATE	TIME	EXPERIENCE

DATE	TIME	EXPERIENCE

DATE	TIME	EXPERIENCE

DATE   **B**=BREAKFAST **L**=LUNCH **D**=DINNER **S**=SNACK

DATE **B**=BREAKFAST **L**=LUNCH **D**=DINNER **S**=SNACK

DATE   **B**=BREAKFAST **L**=LUNCH **D**=DINNER **S**=SNACK

DATE   **B**=BREAKFAST **L**=LUNCH **D**=DINNER **S**=SNACK

DATE   **B**=BREAKFAST **L**=LUNCH **D**=DINNER **S**=SNACK

DATE   **B**=BREAKFAST **L**=LUNCH **D**=DINNER **S**=SNACK

DATE   **B**=BREAKFAST **L**=LUNCH **D**=DINNER **S**=SNACK

DATE   **B**=BREAKFAST **L**=LUNCH **D**=DINNER **S**=SNACK

DATE   **B**=BREAKFAST **L**=LUNCH **D**=DINNER **S**=SNACK

DATE **B**=BREAKFAST **L**=LUNCH **D**=DINNER **S**=SNACK

DATE   **B**=BREAKFAST **L**=LUNCH **D**=DINNER **S**=SNACK

DATE   **B**=BREAKFAST **L**=LUNCH **D**=DINNER **S**=SNACK

DATE | **B**=BREAKFAST **L**=LUNCH **D**=DINNER **S**=SNACK

DATE　　**B**=BREAKFAST　**L**=LUNCH　**D**=DINNER　**S**=SNACK

DATE   **B**=BREAKFAST **L**=LUNCH **D**=DINNER **S**=SNACK

DATE   **B**=BREAKFAST   **L**=LUNCH   **D**=DINNER   **S**=SNACK

DATE   **B**=BREAKFAST **L**=LUNCH **D**=DINNER **S**=SNACK

DATE   **B**=BREAKFAST **L**=LUNCH **D**=DINNER **S**=SNACK

DATE   **B**=BREAKFAST **L**=LUNCH **D**=DINNER **S**=SNACK

DATE   **B**=BREAKFAST **L**=LUNCH **D**=DINNER **S**=SNACK

DATE　　**B**=BREAKFAST　**L**=LUNCH　**D**=DINNER　**S**=SNACK

DATE B=BREAKFAST L=LUNCH D=DINNER S=SNACK

DATE   **B**=BREAKFAST **L**=LUNCH **D**=DINNER **S**=SNACK

DATE	TIME	EXPERIENCE

EMOTIONAL STATE BEFORE MEDITATION

EMOTIONAL STATE AFTER MEDITATION

DATE	TIME	EXPERIENCE

EMOTIONAL STATE BEFORE MEDITATION

EMOTIONAL STATE AFTER MEDITATION

DATE	TIME	EXPERIENCE

EMOTIONAL STATE BEFORE MEDITATION

EMOTIONAL STATE AFTER MEDITATION

DATE	TIME	EXPERIENCE

EMOTIONAL STATE BEFORE MEDITATION

EMOTIONAL STATE AFTER MEDITATION

DATE	TIME	EXPERIENCE

EMOTIONAL STATE BEFORE MEDITATION

EMOTIONAL STATE AFTER MEDITATION

DATE	TIME	EXPERIENCE

EMOTIONAL STATE BEFORE MEDITATION

EMOTIONAL STATE AFTER MEDITATION

DATE	TIME	EXPERIENCE

EMOTIONAL STATE BEFORE MEDITATION

EMOTIONAL STATE AFTER MEDITATION

DATE	TIME	EXPERIENCE

EMOTIONAL STATE BEFORE MEDITATION

EMOTIONAL STATE AFTER MEDITATION

DATE	TIME	EXPERIENCE

EMOTIONAL STATE BEFORE MEDITATION

EMOTIONAL STATE AFTER MEDITATION

DATE	TIME	EXPERIENCE

EMOTIONAL STATE BEFORE MEDITATION

EMOTIONAL STATE AFTER MEDITATION

DATE	TIME	EXPERIENCE

EMOTIONAL STATE BEFORE MEDITATION

EMOTIONAL STATE AFTER MEDITATION

DATE	TIME	EXPERIENCE

EMOTIONAL STATE BEFORE MEDITATION

EMOTIONAL STATE AFTER MEDITATION

DATE	TIME	EXPERIENCE

EMOTIONAL STATE BEFORE MEDITATION

EMOTIONAL STATE AFTER MEDITATION

DATE	TIME	EXPERIENCE

EMOTIONAL STATE BEFORE MEDITATION

EMOTIONAL STATE AFTER MEDITATION

DATE	TIME	EXPERIENCE

EMOTIONAL STATE BEFORE MEDITATION

EMOTIONAL STATE AFTER MEDITATION

DATE	TIME	EXPERIENCE

EMOTIONAL STATE BEFORE MEDITATION

EMOTIONAL STATE AFTER MEDITATION

DATE	TIME	EXPERIENCE

EMOTIONAL STATE BEFORE MEDITATION

EMOTIONAL STATE AFTER MEDITATION

DATE	TIME	EXPERIENCE

EMOTIONAL STATE BEFORE MEDITATION

EMOTIONAL STATE AFTER MEDITATION

DATE	TIME	EXPERIENCE

EMOTIONAL STATE BEFORE MEDITATION

EMOTIONAL STATE AFTER MEDITATION

DATE	TIME	EXPERIENCE

EMOTIONAL STATE BEFORE MEDITATION

EMOTIONAL STATE AFTER MEDITATION

ACKNOWLEDGMENTS

I continue to be infinitely grateful to the talented team at Sterling. It is a gift to collaborate once again! Kate Zimmermann is a consummate professional brimming with talent, creativity, and kindness. I am incredibly fortunate to get to work with her. Thanks so much to the spectacular designers, Elizabeth Mihaltse Lindy and Sharon Jacobs, who made this journal so gorgeous. The sales, distribution, and marketing teams at Sterling are miracle workers. I feel such gratitude when I see one of my books in Whole Foods, Francesca's, Good Earth Trading, or any of the other amazing stores within which you place them.

My literary agent, Lisa Hagan, is one of the kindest, most caring friends I've known. Plus, she is an expert guide in the world of publishing. Every year, she makes my dreams come true and I am forever grateful.

ABOUT THE AUTHOR

Amy Leigh Mercree is a best-selling author, holistic health expert, and medical intuitive. Mercree speaks and teaches internationally, sharing Next Level Healing, Meet Your Guides, Mindfulness Meditation, and Bestseller Bootcamp classes.

Mercree is the author of *The Spiritual Girl's Guide to Dating*, *A Little Bit of Chakras*, *Joyful Living: 101 Ways to Transform Your Spirit & Revitalize Your Life*, *The Chakras and Crystals Cookbook*, *The Compassion Revolution: 30 Days of Living from the Heart*, *A Little Bit of Meditation*, *Essential Oils Handbook*, *Apple Cider Vinegar Handbook*, *A Little Bit of Mindfulness*, *The Mood Book: Crystals, Oils, and Rituals to Elevate Your Spirit*, *A Little Bit of Goddess: An Introduction to the Divine Feminine*, and *100 Days to Calm*.

Mercree has been featured in *Glamour* magazine; *Women's Health, Inc.* magazine; *Shape*; *The Huffington Post*; *Your Tango*; *Soul and Spirit* magazine; *Mind Body Green*; *Hello Giggles*; *Reader's Digest*; *O, The Oprah Magazine*; *Forbes*; *First for Women*; *Country Living*; *Bustle*; *Elite Daily*; *Thrive Global*; CBS; NBC; FOX; and many more.

Mercree is fast becoming one of the most quoted women on the web. See what all the buzz is about @AmyLeighMercree on social media.

To download your FREE mindfulness tool kit and find peace amid your hectic brain life now, go to **www.amyleighmercree.com/mindfulnesstoolkit** —password **MINDFUL.**